Everything
BIRD

What Kids Really Want to Know About Birds

by
Cherie
Winner

NORTHWORD
Minnetonka, Minnesota

Edited by Kristen McCurry
Designed by Lois A. Rainwater
Design concept by Michele Lanci-Altomare

Text © 2007 by Cherie Winner

NorthWord

Books for Young Readers
11571 K-Tel Drive
Minnetonka, MN 55343
www.tnkidsbooks.com

Photographs © 2007 provided by:

All photos Shutterstock except for the following:
Deborah Allen: p. 60 (top left); Daniel Dempster/Bruce Coleman: p. 45 (top); Digi-
tial Vision: pp. 6 (bottom), 7, 8, 20, 33, 51 (bird outline);
Tim Fitzharris/Minden Pictures: p. 21 (bottom);
JupiterImages Corporation: p. 55 (bottom); William Leaman/Alamy: p. 45 (bottom);
Phototake Inc./Alamy: p. 22; Tom Vezo: pp. 41 (top), 58 (left);
Dave Watts/Alamy: p. 59.

Library of Congress Cataloging-in-Publication Data

Winner, Cherie.
Everything bird : what kids really want to know about birds /
by Cherie Winner.
p. cm.
Includes bibliographical references.
ISBN-13: 978-1-55971-962-9 (hc)
ISBN-13: 978-1-55971-963-6 (sc)
1. Birds--Miscellanea--Juvenile literature. I. Title.

QL676.2.W56 2007
598--dc22   2006021913

Printed in Singapore

Acknowledgments

THE AUTHOR THANKS the students at St. Francis of Assisi School in West Des Moines, Iowa, and all the other kids who have shared their questions, stories, and ideas.

Dedication

For my cousin Peggy,
who loves to watch birds.
—C. W.

contents

What do Canada geese, chickadees, and flamingos have in common?

introduction

ONE OF THE BEST THINGS ABOUT WRITING NATURE
books for kids is that I get to visit schools and talk with
students about the kinds of animals and plants they're
interested in. On every visit, somebody asks me what my
favorite animal is. I've never figured out how to answer
that question. I love all animals, and it's tough to pick just
one as a favorite.

But I might have a favorite group of animals—
birds. They're quick and smart, beautiful and graceful,
and they're great singers. Best of all, they fly.

And that's just the beginning. Almost any cool
thing you can think of, there's probably a bird that does
it. There are birds that dive, birds that dance, birds that
run faster than you can ride your bike, and birds that eat
snakes. Okay, maybe that last thing wouldn't be much
fun. But it's still cool that birds do it.

Not that everything birds do is wonderful. Blue
jays bully other birds. Starlings and Canada geese can be
a nuisance. A rooster crowing at 4 a.m. is a lousy neighbor.
And I don't know anyone who likes getting hit with bird
poop. But what would a spring morning be without the
songbirds chirping? And every pond needs a few dabbling
ducks to provide entertainment!

There are so many different birds with so many
different talents, but what do they all have in common?
What makes a bird a bird?

What makes a bird a bird?

The main thing that sets birds apart from other animals is that all birds have feathers covering most of their body. No other kind of animal has feathers. Feathers do many jobs. They keep a bird warm. The colors and patterns of a bird's feathers give important signals to other birds. They show whether the bird is male or female, young or adult, ready to breed or ready to migrate. Feathers also allow a bird to fly. Without feathers, a bird flapping its bare wings wouldn't get any farther off the ground than you would by flapping your arms.

That brings up another thing that's special about birds. They all have wings instead of arms—even the ones, like penguins and ostriches, that don't fly.

Drab and dull or shimmering and bright, feathers make birds different from all other living things.

Why do ostriches and penguins have wings if they don't fly?

It does seem weird, doesn't it? If you were designing an ostrich from scratch, you wouldn't give it wings. You'd give it front legs it could run on, or arms and paws it could use for gathering food or taking care of its babies.

Chickens don't fly well. Humans have bred them to be so heavy (more meat!) that their small wings can barely lift them off the ground.

But ostriches, emus, and other flightless birds are stuck with wings because they inherited them from ancestors that did fly. They also inherited the ability to get food, make nests, and do other tasks by using their bills or feet.

Some flightless birds use their wings for something other than flying. Penguins flap their wings to power themselves through the water. When ostriches are on their nest, they spread their wings to shade their eggs from the desert sun.

ostrich

Some birds *can* fly, but prefer to run. Roadrunners, birds that live in the southwestern United States and Mexico, are much faster on the ground than in the air. Roadrunners have been clocked running 23 miles (37 km) per hour. That's fast enough to catch snakes and lizards. If you've ever tried to catch a snake or lizard, you know—that's fast!

How do birds fly?

Birds can fly because their wings are just the right shape to "catch air" and create what is called lift. You can see this happening when a seagull gets ready to take off. It faces into the wind and holds out its wings. The wind lifts it up.

You can feel lift if you hold out the flaps of your jacket on a windy day. The lift doesn't carry you into the air because you are too heavy. Lift gets birds off the ground because birds weigh so little. No part of a bird is heavy, not even its bones. Many of the bones in their wings and legs are hollow, and many of

A Franklin's gull spreads its wings to catch enough air for lift-off.

the bones in their spine, chest, and pelvis are fused together to make a body that is incredibly strong and light.

Birds don't even have teeth and big jaw muscles, which would make their heads too heavy for flight. Instead, they have a lightweight beak and no teeth.

Wings can be short and broad, like the mallard's (above), or long and thin, like the Northern gannet's (below).

If birds don't have teeth, how do they chew their food?

They don't. Not with their mouths, anyway. Birds swallow their food in big bites. First it goes into an organ called the crop. Then it moves to the gizzard, which is surrounded by powerful muscles that grind up the food. Some birds swallow pebbles or sand to help grind food in the gizzard. So you could say that birds "chew" their food in the gizzard.

This puffin will swallow the fish whole, and let his gizzard grind them up.

Are really big beaks heavy, like the toucan's?

How heavy are your fingernails? Bird beaks have a few thin bones inside them, but the part we see is made of the same stuff that your fingernails are made of. It's a protein called keratin. So bird beaks are very light. Even toucan bills don't weigh much. The toco toucan has the biggest bill of any toucan. A big toco is about 2 feet (61 cm) long and weighs just over a pound (0.5 kg). Its beak is 7.5 inches (19 cm) long and weighs less than an ounce (25 g)!

A toucan's beak isn't as dangerous as it looks. The bird uses it to pluck fruit from tree branches.

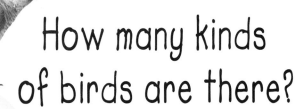

How many kinds of birds are there?

There are about 10,000 species, or kinds, of birds in the world today. They range in size from the bee hummingbird, which is about the size of your thumb, to the ostrich, which is as tall as a horse. They live in almost every habitat on Earth.

We can't say exactly how many species there are, because the number keeps changing. It goes up when scientists discover species we didn't know about before. Finding new species doesn't happen often, but in 2005, scientists exploring a remote jungle in New Guinea found new species of butterflies, frogs, palm trees, and a bird they called a honeyeater.

Unfortunately, it's more common for the number of species to go down. That happens when species die out, or go extinct. Almost one-eighth of all the bird species on Earth are in danger of becoming extinct. In the United States, about 40 species are endangered. They include the California condor, whooping crane, piping plover, and red-cockaded woodpecker. Many people are trying to save these birds, because once a species goes extinct, it is gone forever.

Why do birds go extinct? Can't they just fly away from their problems?

Birds can take to the air to escape from a coyote or other predator. But flying away doesn't solve all their problems.

What if they can't fly? Dodos were turkey-sized birds that lived on an island in the Indian Ocean a few hundred years ago. They didn't fly. They didn't need to. They ate food they found on the ground, they nested on the ground, and the island had no predators big enough to attack them. Then people came to the island. Sailors landed there in 1507, and soon found that they could get tasty meat by walking right up to a dodo and killing it. The dodos had never been attacked before, so they had never learned to run away. In less than 200 years, the dodos were all gone.

California condors
face many problems.
They've lost their habitat,
been hunted and poisoned,
and sometimes crash into power lines.
Scientists are breeding them in captivity to try to save
them, but the species is still endangered. Only about
200 condors live in the wild today.

Like many other raptors, bald eagles suffer when forests are cut down, because they need tall trees in which to build their nests. But their biggest threat came from an insecticide called DDT. Bald eagles nearly died out because DDT caused their egg-shells to be so thin that they broke before the chicks could hatch out.

What if hunters shoot the birds every time they try to fly away? When European settlers first came to America, huge flocks of passenger pigeons lived in the Eastern and Midwestern parts of the country. There were so many that they covered half the sky when they flew over. People hunted them. Nobody thought they could ever kill so many passenger pigeons that the species would disappear, but that's what happened. The last passenger pigeon died in a zoo in 1914.

What if a bird's home has disappeared? This is a problem for many of the bird species that are in trouble today. Prairie chickens need wild grasslands with open areas where they can gather in spring for their mating rituals. Over the past 200 years, as the prairie has been turned into farmland and cities, prairie chickens have lost almost all of their former breeding areas. Now they are endangered.

This greater prairie chicken male is in courtship display.

Were birds around in the time of dinosaurs?

The birds we see today were not around then, but their ancestors were. Birds probably evolved from dinosaurs. They have similar bones and other features. In fact, some biologists think birds are so much like dinosaurs that they ARE dinosaurs!

Almost every year, scientists find new fossils of animals that were like dinosaurs in some ways and like birds in others. They ran on two legs and had small, simple feathers that probably helped them stay warm.

The most famous "early bird" is Archaeopteryx (ar-kee-OP-te-riks). It lived 150 million years ago. Its name means "ancient wings." This bird was about the size of a crow. It had feathers on its wings and tail. The rest of its body was covered with scales, and it had teeth. It probably could climb up trees and glide down, but it couldn't take off from the ground.

Why do flamingos have backward knees?

Flamingos have the same kind of knees as other birds—and none of them are backward! When we look at a bird, what we think are its knees are actually its ankles.

Birds stand on their toes. The rest of the foot is off the ground. The first joint we see above the toes is the ankle. The little knob that points backward there—the one that looks like it's where the knee should be—is like your heel. The knee is up near the body, so we don't often see it. It points forward just like our knees do.

Can an owl really turn its head all the way around?

An owl can turn its head to look almost straight behind it. This helps it watch for possible prey over a wide area, without moving its whole body and letting prey know it is there. But when the owl wants to look forward again, it has to turn its head back the same way it came. If it tries to turn in a full circle—ouch!

This owl chick has baby feathers, but it already has the remarkable eyes that will help it be a great hunter when it grows up.

What do birds eat?

You name it, there's probably a bird that eats it—bugs, slugs, frogs, fish, seeds, sap, and even other birds.

One bird doesn't eat all those things. Each kind of bird eats a certain kind of food. Some eat different things in different seasons. Sparrows eat insects in summer and seeds in winter.

You can usually tell what a bird eats by looking at its bill. Finches have a stout, strong bill they use to crack open tough seeds. Hummingbirds have a needle-like bill they use to reach deep inside flowers to sip out the

Birds of prey need sharp talons to grab prey and tear meat, but songbird chicks just need a mouth big enough to swallow the juicy tidbits their parents bring.

nectar. Herons have a long bill they use to spear fish and frogs in shallow water. Flamingos have a bill with many fine ridges on the inside, like a comb, that they use to filter algae and small mollusks out of the water.

Birds of prey such as hawks, eagles, and owls have strong, curved bills they use to rip meat from the mice, snakes, fish, or other animals they catch. They also have long, sharp talons, or claws, to grab and hold their prey.

Why are vultures so ugly?

Vultures don't have feathers on their head and upper neck. They have bare skin, which is usually red and wrinkly.

To say why they look like that, we have to talk about the gross stuff they eat. Are you ready? Vultures eat meat from animals they find that have already died. A lot of the animals have been dead long enough that they have started to rot. Vultures reach way inside the oozy, smelly body to get the tastiest bits of food. If they had feathers on their head and neck, the feathers would become covered with stinky goo. It's hard for birds to clean their head and neck, so for vultures it's better not to have feathers there at all. The gooey stuff doesn't stick well to plain skin.

And remember, to us they're ugly, but to other vultures they look just fine!

How do birds know to fly south in fall?

Birds know to start flying south when the days get shorter and the temperature drops. They know when it's time to fly back north when the days get longer again and the temperature warms up. They know which way to go partly by instinct, or inborn knowledge, and partly by learning the route during their first migration.

Biologists have found that birds use many clues to tell which way is which. Most birds migrate at night. They check the stars to figure out which direction to go. Canada geese and some other birds migrate during the day. They check the position of the sun. Many migrating birds also use an internal compass that senses the Earth's magnetic field. Their compass is so accurate they can find their way even if it's so cloudy that they can't see the sun or stars.

How far do birds migrate? How long does it take them?

It depends on the kind of bird and where it lives. Many birds don't migrate at all! Most woodpeckers and cardinals stay in the same area all year. They may live their whole lives within a few miles (km) of where they were hatched. Meadowlarks and blue jays may stay put, or they may migrate to areas with more food for the winter. They might decide based on whether they can find enough food or warm enough shelter for the winter, or they might decide based on things we don't know about yet.

Many species migrate only a few hundred miles (km)—just far enough to reach a place where they will be safe and have plenty to eat during the winter.

Migrating birds, like these snow geese, often gather in huge flocks before starting their journey.

Then there are the long-distance migrators. Some shorebirds go from northern Canada all the way to the southern end of South America—a trip of more than 8,000 miles (12,800 km)! The all-time champion migrator is the arctic tern. It nests in the far north, sometimes when there's still snow on the ground. Once the chicks can take care of themselves, the terns head south. They fly all the way to Antarctica, nearly 11,000 miles (17,600 km) away. In spring they go back to the Arctic to breed again.

An arctic tern grabs a snack before continuing its journey.

This might sound as if terns fly from one cold place to another. Actually, the Arctic and Antarctic have mild temperatures when the terns are there. The really cool thing is that because of the way the Earth tilts, those areas have sunlight almost all day when the terns are there. The only time they have dark nights is when they're migrating.

Terns don't rush. Their journey takes them two or three months. They stop at places where they can find food. Other birds, like geese, often make their trips in one long flight. Snow geese migrate from northern Canada to the coast of Louisiana, a trip of about 1,700 miles (2,735 km), without stopping. One flock of snow geese made the trip in 60 hours, which means they went at about 28 miles (45 km) per hour. That might not sound super-fast, but even a car couldn't do that for 60 hours straight without stopping for gas!

Are birds smart?

Yes, birds are pretty smart. Some are smarter than others. Some are even smarter than dogs!

Birds do a lot of things by instinct. That means they know how to do certain things soon after they hatch. They have inborn knowledge. For example, gull chicks don't have to learn how to ask for food from their parents. Adult gulls have a red spot on each side of their bill. When a chick pecks at the red spot, the parent regurgitates food for it. Chicks don't have to learn to peck at red spots; they just do it by instinct.

But birds don't do everything by instinct. They also learn new skills and adapt, or adjust, to new situations. Robins, red-winged blackbirds, and other songbirds recognize the voice of a neighboring bird even if the neighbor starts singing a completely new kind of song. Chickadees

A chickadee looks over the goodies at a bird feeder.

store thousands of seeds in different places to eat during the winter—and remember where most of them are.

Parrots and mockingbirds are great mimics. They can imitate all kinds of sounds. That's how parrots learn to "talk." The cool thing is, parrots seem to know what the sounds mean. A well-educated parrot will say "Hello" when you come into its room and "Good-bye" when you leave it.

HELLO!

Besides parrots, the smartest birds are members of the crow family, which includes crows, ravens, and jays. They can figure out how to open containers and how to use a stick to reach food inside a tube. On intelligence tests they often do better than dogs at tasks like counting and figuring out how to get food that is out of reach. Way to go, birds!

"MENU, PLEASE!"

How many different sounds can one bird make?

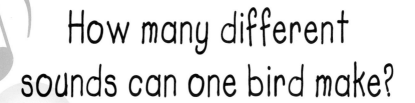

It depends on the kind of bird and what time of year it is. Many birds make songs, which are mostly sung by males during the breeding season. Birds start out with a few songs they know by instinct. As they grow up, they learn new songs. Some learn dozens of new songs every spring. A male brown thrasher may sing thousands of different songs! Knowing many songs is a way to impress females and win a mate.

All birds make calls, which don't change much during the bird's life. Calls are usually shorter than songs, and carry

Name that tune! This brown thrasher might know more songs than you can put on an iPod.

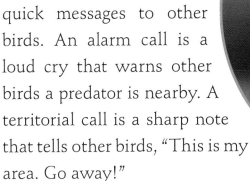

quick messages to other birds. An alarm call is a loud cry that warns other birds a predator is nearby. A territorial call is a sharp note that tells other birds, "This is my area. Go away!"

Birds also make other sounds. Swans hiss to warn away intruders. Male ruffed grouse attract females by drumming on a fallen log with their wings. Woodpeckers pound on trees, houses, and power poles to let other birds know they are there.

When they're not busy making a nest in a saguaro cactus, gila woodpeckers chatter a lot and drum on dead trees. They are VERY noisy birds!

Why are cardinals red?

Bird colors almost always tell other birds (and us!) something about the bird. With cardinals, the bright red means the bird is an adult male. Females and young birds have reddish brown feathers. In cardinals, as in many other birds, the males are more colorful than the females. It is up to the females to choose which male they will mate with, and having bright colors helps the males attract a mate.

In many bird species, the males and females look almost the same, but the male still has more color. He might have a bright splash of red or yellow on his face or neck. For example, male red-shafted flickers have a red "mustache" the females don't have.

female

male

In some species, the males have bits of color hidden under covering feathers. Male red-winged blackbirds have red patches and a yellow stripe on the front of each wing. When the bird is just standing there, we can see the yellow stripe but very little of the red. But if another male redwing comes along, the first male will lower its chest and lift its wings to show off its wing patches. Then we say he is displaying.

A display is a movement that birds use to give a strong message to other birds—in this case, "Off my turf!" Other displays say "Be my mate" or "Don't crowd me when I'm eating."

A red-winged blackbird shows off his shoulder patches, and a great egret displays to win a mate.

Do all birds make nests?

Amazingly, they don't. All birds lay eggs, but a few kinds of birds, such as ring-necked pheasants, just lay them on a bare patch of ground. Sometimes the mother pheasant scrapes the dirt to make a shallow bowl shape to keep her eggs from rolling away, but that's it.

Most birds do make nests, and they have found many different ways to do it. Orioles and weaver birds weave basket-like nests that hang from branches. Kingfishers dig tunnels up to 10 feet (3 m) long into stream banks, and lay their eggs in a chamber at the end of the tunnel. Every species has its own special way of making a safe place for its eggs and chicks.

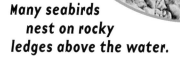

Many seabirds nest on rocky ledges above the water.

A piping plover (top) lays her eggs on a sandy beach. Great crested grebes (bottom) make a nest that floats!

Ducklings swim beside their parents soon after hatching (top) while songbird chicks start life naked and blind (bottom).

How many chicks do mother and father birds have every year?

It depends on the species and where they live. Some, like condors and albatrosses, reproduce very slowly. They usually lay just one egg every year or two. Other birds lay a lot more eggs. Some that live in areas with long summers raise more than one clutch, or group of chicks, every year. After one clutch of chicks flies away to live on their own, the parents get busy with another group of eggs. Doves lay just one or two eggs, but they nest up to five times every year. Tiny chickadees usually raise one or two clutches of chicks every year. Each clutch usually has from 5 to 10 babies, but sometimes as many as 19! The champion egg-layers may be the cowbirds, which can lay more than 40 eggs every year!

Waved albatross parents raise just one chick each year.

How can cowbirds raise so many babies?

They get other birds to do the job for them. Really! Biologists think they started doing this because they followed herds of buffalo that roamed across the prairie. As the buffalo grazed, they stirred up delicious insects the cowbirds ate. Since the cowbirds were always on the move, they were never in one place long enough to raise babies. So they got other birds to do it for them.

Here's how it works: The female cowbird finds a nest of some other species, and waits until the parent goes out to find food. Then the cowbird rolls one of the other eggs out of the nest, and lays her own egg in its place! The cowbird egg is often much larger than the host eggs. It also develops faster, so the cowbird chick is the first one to hatch out. It gets most of the attention and food from its new "parents." It may even kick the smaller chicks out of the nest. This is obviously very bad for the host birds.

Nowadays, we no longer have buffalo herds crossing the country. But the cowbirds are still doing their thing, sometimes causing great harm to other species of birds.

Kirtland's warblers were nearly wiped out by cowbirds who laid eggs in their nests, resulting in the death of the warblers' own babies.

Most birds take good care of their babies, don't they?

Yes, most birds are great parents. They feed their chicks, keep them warm, protect them from predators, and help them learn to fly.

Some bird babies need more care than others. Songbirds, such as robins and sparrows, are

These chicks have a lot more growing to do. Their eyes aren't open yet, but their mouths sure are!

helpless when they hatch out of their eggs. They have just a few wispy feathers and their eyes aren't open yet. They can't walk or fly. They can't even stand. They depend on their parents for everything.

Other bird babies, like ducklings and chicken chicks, have a full coat of fluffy feathers. They can see, eat on their own, and walk. Baby ducks and geese can swim. But they still need their parents to help them stay warm and find where the best food is.

What is an owl pellet?

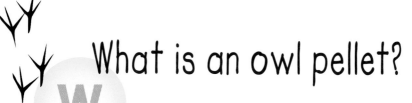

When an owl catches dinner, such as a mouse, it doesn't delicately peel off the meat. It swallows the whole mouse. But it can't digest the whole mouse. In the owl's gizzard, the mouse meat gets digested. The bones, teeth, and hair get smushed together into a tight pellet the owl then barfs out.

By the way, owls aren't the only birds that barf up pellets. Other birds of prey do it, too. Owls are just the most famous.

Pellets from this spectacled owl might contain bones of frogs, birds, or even a skunk!

Do woodpeckers ever get a headache from hammering on wood?

Amazingly, they don't. Or at least, we think they don't. They keep hammering, so it must not hurt too badly. The bones in their head, neck, and back are heavier and stronger than in most birds, and they have very strong muscles that help absorb the shock.

It's a good thing, too, because woodpeckers hammer on wood a LOT. They do it to reach insects that live inside the trees, to excavate a hole in which to make their nest, and to communicate with other woodpeckers—like using drum signals.

Why is bird poop so runny?

Instead of getting rid of solid waste (poop) and liquid waste (urine) separately, as mammals do, birds mix the two. So the whitish green splats on your bike or your family's car contain both poop and pee. Ewww.

How many feathers does a bird have?

It depends on the size of the bird and where it lives. Hummingbirds, which are tiny and live in warm places, have about 1,000 feathers. Swans, which are large and paddle around on chilly lakes, have more than 25,000.

Not all feathers are the same. Long, stiff flight feathers are on the wings. Shorter feathers cover most of the body. Beneath them, like a layer of long underwear, are fluffy down feathers that keep the bird warm.

One feather alone feels like it weighs next to nothing, but all of a bird's feathers together weigh twice as much as the bird's bones!

Snowy egrets (above) have long plume feathers they use in courtship displays.

Why do birds pick at their feathers?

To keep them clean and smooth. The picking is called preening. At least once every day, a bird preens by running its bill through its feathers to pick off dirt and bugs. The great blue heron has a special claw with ridges and grooves on it that it uses especially for preening its head and neck feathers. The claw is like a built-in comb!

Even with preening, feathers eventually get ragged and torn. They don't keep the bird warm as well as they once did, and they slow the bird down when it flies. So birds replace their feathers once or twice a year, in a process called molting.

Be sure to get EVERY spot clean!

52

Birds don't molt all of the feathers at the same time. If they did, we'd see naked birds running around! Some, like ducks, lose most of their flight feathers at one time. Until their new flight feathers grow in, they are grounded. They look for a place, such as an island, where they will be safe from predators until they are able to fly again.

A tricolored heron uses its claws to preen feathers on its head and neck.

How do I bring more birds to my own yard?

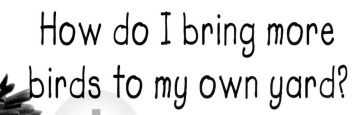

Look at your yard from a bird's point of view. Is there anything to eat? Is there clean water to drink? Are there trees or posts where they can perch and feel safe from cats and other dangerous creatures? If you provide these things, your yard will be a favorite spot for the birds in your area.

When seeds fall to the ground underneath your bird feeder, leave them there. They attract other

> *Birds look for plants that make tasty seeds or attract yummy insects.*

birds, such as juncos and doves, which prefer to eat on the ground. And remember that not all birds eat seeds. A small patch of wildflowers will be a favorite spot for sparrows, flycatchers, and others that eat insects.

Besides having trees and bushes nearby where birds can hide if a predator comes along, check your windows. Birds sometimes hurt themselves badly, or even die, by flying into windows. They probably can't see the glass, because it reflects the trees and sky. Tape a bird-shaped cutout on any large windows to help them see the glass.

Do birds make good pets?

Some kinds of birds make wonderful pets! Parakeets, canaries, cockatiels, and some finches are popular pet birds. If you take care of them right, they will be your cheerful, beautiful friends for many years.

Wild birds, on the other hand, do not make good pets. Some people feed geese and ducks that visit ponds near their home. They are trying to help the birds, but they might actually be hurting them. "People food" is not good for wild birds. It's also not good for the birds to depend on humans for their food. They need to be able to find food on their own, in the wild. Trying to make friends with these birds can be dangerous for people, too. A goose can give you a bite you will never forget! Just remember they are wild animals and should be respected as wild animals. Enjoy their beauty but keep your distance.

Cockatiels
are beautiful
AND smart.

What's the coolest thing birds do?

Everyone has a favorite, but I love the way the American dipper gets its food. Dippers are small gray birds that live along streams in the western United States. A dipper dips its head underwater to look for plump insects that live in the stream. When it sees something that looks tasty, it hops into the water and walks along the bottom to reach it. Then it nabs the bug, hops out of the water onto a rock, and chows down.

Another really cool thing is the way male shrikes attract a mate. They don't strut and sing. Instead, they show off how well they would provide for a family. Each

male chooses a thorn bush or a stretch of barbed-wire fence that will be his "gallery." He gathers bugs, string, bits of paper, and anything else that catches his eye. He sticks each item on a thorn or barb. One shrike can display more than 100 items! When female shrikes see a big gallery of goodies, they know the male who made it will be a good mate who will bring plenty of food to their chicks.

Those are just two of the cool things birds do, but I don't know about calling them "the coolest." The more birds you see, the more cool things you see them do. That's the great thing about birds—no matter how much you know about them or how often you see them, they always give you something new to marvel at. Birds truly are amazing creatures!

Frogmouth

Hoopoe

Bee eaters

A hoopoe flares its crest, a frogmouth looks
surprised, and a group of bee eaters enjoys dinner.

weird bird names

- Hoopoe – This bird was named for the sound it makes: "Oop-oop-oop!" The Eurasion hoopoe has one of the best scientific names ever: Upupa epops (OO-pah-pah EE-pops). Hoopoes are fun to watch. When they're upset or excited they show a tall crest on their heads, and when they fly they zigzag like a giant butterfly.

- Frogmouth – When these birds open their short beaks and wide mouths, they look a bit like frogs. They have big heads and eyes, and they hunt just before sunrise and after sunset. They sit on a low branch and watch for creepy-crawlies such as centipedes and scorpions.

- Bee eater – These are birds that specialize in eating honey-bees. They only nab bees that are flying. A bee sitting on a flower is safe from them. When they catch a bee, they carry it to a perch in a tree. They bash and rub the bee against the tree to get rid of the venom in the bee's stinger. Then they gobble up their treat.

- Blue-footed booby – One look at this bird, and the "blue-footed" part of their name makes sense. But why are they "boobies?" They live on islands near the western coast of South America, where they never had to worry about predators on the ground. Like dodos, they never developed any fear of humans or other land predators. When sailors from Europe landed on the islands, they were able to walk right up to the birds and capture or kill them. The name "booby" comes from the Spanish word "bobo," which means "stupid one"–an unfair name if ever there was one!

resources

BOOKS

BENT, ARTHUR CLEVELAND. *Life Histories of North American Woodpeckers.* Bloomington: Indiana University Press, 1992.

GIBSON, GRAEME. *The Bedside Book of Birds: An Avian Miscellany.* Nan A. Talese, 2005.

JOHNSGARD, PAUL A. *Crane Music: A Natural History of American Cranes.* Washington, D.C.: Smithsonian Institution Press, 1991. Reprinted, Lincoln: University of Nebraska Press, 1997.

LINCOLN, FREDERICK C., STEVEN R. PETERSON, and JOHN L. ZIMMERMAN. *Migration of Birds.* Washington, D.C.: U.S. Fish and Wildlife Service Circular #16, 1998.

SIBLEY, DAVID ALLEN. *The Sibley Guide to Bird Life and Behavior.* New York: Alfred A. Knopf, 2001.

SIBLEY, DAVID ALLEN. *The Sibley Guide to Birds.* New York: Alfred A. Knopf, 2000.

SIBLEY, DAVID ALLEN. *Sibley's Birding Basics.* New York: Alfred A. Knopf, 2002.

TUDGE, COLIN. *The Variety of Life: A survey and a celebration of all the creatures that have ever lived.* Oxford: Oxford University Press, 2000.

WEINER, JONATHAN. *The Beak of the Finch: A Story of Evolution in Our Time.* New York: Alfred A. Knopf, 1994.

WEB SITES

http://nationalzoo.si.edu/Animals/Birds/ForKids/default.cfm
At this site you can play bird games, print out pictures of birds to color, find world record birds, and watch the flamingo cam or kiwi cam.

www.wildbirds.com/kids_teaching.htm
Go to this site to find out more about attracting, identifying, and photographing birds. It also has lots of information about nests and eggs.

www.birds.cornell.edu
Check out the bird of the week and see all the chick-raising action through nest cams at this website from the Cornell Laboratory of Ornithology. It also has recordings of bird songs and calls you can listen to.

http://vireo.acnatsci.org//index.html
Find photos of chicks and adults of almost any bird you can think of at this site.

http://magma.nationalgeographic.com/ngm/cranecam/about.html
Watch videos of sandhill cranes dancing, feeding, and migrating through Nebraska's Platte River valley at this website from the National Geographic Society.

www.birdsource.org/gbbc/
Once you have a bird feeder or find a good place to go bird watching near home, go to this site and find out how to join the Great Backyard Bird Count to help biologists keep track of birds across the country.

www.audubon.org/bird/at_home
The Audubon Society website has photos, maps, and the latest information on endangered species of birds.

www.enature.com/birding/index.asp
At this site you can find the best places to go bird watching near your hometown. Try out the special feature called "Hawk Watch" to learn where to see wild hawks in action.

www.owlpages.com/index.php
If you love owls, you'll love this site. It's filled with photos, recordings of owl hoots, owl stories, information about owls, and owls in the news.

www.npwrc.usgs.gov/resource/tools/duckdist/duckdist.htm
This site, called Ducks at a Distance, gives you pictures and descriptions to help you identify puddle ducks, diving ducks, geese, and swans.

www.geocities.com/allaboutparrots
If you have a pet parrot or parakeet, or if you think you'd like to have one, this is the site for you. Learn about what they eat, how much space they need, how to keep them healthy, and how to teach them to do tricks.

About the Author

CHERIE WINNER is a science writer for *Washington State Magazine* and also writes science and nature books for children. Her favorite subjects are animals and plants, and the people who study them. Several of her books have been named Outstanding Science Trade Books for Children. Dr. Winner has taught college classes, done research on salamanders, and worked as a newspaper reporter. Nowadays, when she isn't writing, she enjoys gardening and spending time with her small cat, Smudge, and her large dog, Harper.